BRITISH RAILWAYS

PAST and PRESENT

COLOUR SPECIAL

Third selection

KEADBY, LINCOLNSHIRE: The King George V bridge on the former Great Central Doncaster-Scunthorpe line was built to cross the River Trent and was to a design patented by the Scherzer Rolling Lift Bridge Company of the USA. The eastern section of the bridge was designed to lift to allow the passage of river traffic and this facility remained in use until 1956. The bridge also carries the busy A18 road. In the 'past' picture, Gresley 'O2/3' 2-8-0 No 63957 heads east under the former lifting section of the bridge with a coal train for Frodingham on 25 October 1961.

   Apart from the removal of the siding in the foreground, little has changed in the spring of 1993 as Class 37 No 37719 crosses with an eastbound freight. There are more Lincolnshire views in the final section of this book.
J. F. Oxley/Roger Hill

BRITISH RAILWAYS
PAST and PRESENT

COLOUR SPECIAL
Third selection

Including special 'appetite-whetter' photo-features on the
Ffestiniog and Welsh Highland Railways, and the railways of Lincolnshire

Past and Present

Past & Present Publishing Ltd

First published in November 1995

The colour material is that added to the new editions of 'British Railways Past and Present' Nos 10, 13 and 16, and that contained in Nos 23, 25, 26, 27 and the 'Past and Present Special' on the Tarka Trail.

British Library Cataloguing in Publication Data

A catalogue record for this book is available from the British Library

ISBN 1 85895 093 7

Past & Present Publishing Ltd
Unit 5
Home Farm Close
Church Street
Wadenhoe
Peterborough PE8 5TE
Tel/fax (01832) 720440

Printed and bound in Great Britain

INTRODUCTION

This third collection of colour and black & white 'past and present' photographs provides perhaps an even more varied selection than the previous two volumes - from the wilds of Snowdonia to the heart of London, from a long-distance footpath in Devon converted from former railway lines to the industrial counties of the Midlands.

The photo-features that 'top and tail' the collected colour sections have been specially assembled by the respective authors of two forthcoming 'Past and Present' volumes, to whet your appetite for delights to come! A 'Past and Present Special' on the Ffestiniog and Welsh Highland Railways, by well-known railway author and photographer John Stretton, is due to be published in the spring of 1996. It follows similar successful preserved line 'Specials' on the Paignton & Dartmouth Steam Railway and the Severn Valley Railway; several more titles are in preparation.

In the regular series, No 27 covers the railways of Lincolnshire, and authors Roger Hill and Carey Vessey have chosen 15 pairs additional to those selected for the book. They amply demonstrate the enormous variety of railways in England's second largest county.

Will Adams
Editor

FFESTINIOG AND
WELSH HIGHLAND RAILWAYS

John Stretton

PORTHMADOG (I): During the period of the Welsh Highland Railway, the Ffestiniog Railway's Harbour station was generally known as 'Portmadoc Old', and when the preservationists came to it in 1952 it was in an extremely dilapidated condition. Some of the tremendous renovation work undertaken by them and their successors can be seen in this view, taken in August 1963 during the Centenary year, not least in the quality of coach restoration.

While recognisable as the same view, the herculean efforts at further development and progress by the railway can be witnessed in this shot from 4 June 1995. The main station roof-line has lost its chimneys, but has gained dormer windows, partly hiding the tree behind, and this building has been joined to the old goods shed by a brand new erection, housing the cafe and museum. The trackwork has seen some re-alignment and the trains are now much longer, filling the whole platform length; the only 'reverse' progress is the signs of ageing on coach 16 and the disappearance of television aerials on the houses on the main road in the background.
Jon Marsh/John Stretton

PORTHMADOG (2): Stalwart of the Ffestiniog in its early preservation years was 1863-vintage England 0-4-0T *Prince*, after an overhaul taking 18 years in total (begun in 1937, a new boiler was ordered but not delivered until 1945 shortly before the railway closed, and it was left to the enthusiasts in the early 1950s to fit it and complete the work, in August 1955!). On 26 September 1959, by now sharing duties with other locomotives, the little engine draws into Portmadoc station off the mile-long Cob with a train from Tan-y-Bwlch; evidence of the amount of weeding and general tidying-up can be judged by the clean-looking track and surrounding areas.

Over virtually the whole of its 130-odd year life, *Prince* has seen modifications, change and rebuilding, and the process still continues, with plans for further amendments to the tender design. That this has already received attention can be judged by comparison between these two views, showing the major alteration for oil burning, the addition of a buffer plate and general sophistication for modern-day running, including the highly attractive livery. Other changes are the amended trackwork, including the disappearance of fishplates and chairs; the office building to replace the Britannia Works offices, closed in 1965; and the greater number of levers to cope with the new points. *E. R. Morten/John Stretton*

BOSTON LODGE: A shot of real Ffestiniog Railway history from 1970. 1893-vintage Hunslet *Linda* had been converted to a 2-4-0ST tender engine earlier that year, from the 0-4-0T that she was when first on the railway in 1962, and she is still coal-burning - evidenced by the skilful way the fireman is depositing the fuel into the tender(!); she was converted to oil-firing the next year. In the background is the 'long shed'. A piece of original FR construction, this served as a running shed for over 30 years in preservation, but was becoming increasingly deteriorated, necessitating its demolition in 1988.

The trackwork is the only clue to this being the same vantage point, although presumably old habits die hard, as the wagon roads are common to both views, but power generation is decidedly more modern in the 'present' one! With the long shed gone, the view to the sea is unimpaired and locomotives standing on the pit (once housed within the shed) now have no protection from the elements. On 4 June 1995 Double Fairlie *Merddin Emrys* receives end-of-day attention after coming on shed from working its last train down from Blaenau Ffestiniog. *Jon Marsh/John Stretton*

MINFFORDD is the first 'full-time' station out of Porthmadog, but for the first few years of restoration it saw no trains, with the tracks being heavily overgrown. After much work, services returned to the station from 19 May 1956, but with the trackbed liberally carpeted with grass. The railway regained access to higher up the line, to Tan-y-Bwlch, in 1958, and in this view of a cabless and square-tanked *Merddin Emrys* leaving with a down service in 1961, the attentions of the track gangs can be judged.

When the railway finally reached the northern terminus at Blaenau Ffestiniog and increased the level of services, some not running the whole length, it became necessary for trains to pass at Minffordd, hence on 4 June 1995 *Merddin Emrys* has 'crossed' to what is now the down line. As can be seen, many changes have also been made to the locomotive, bringing it back to near-original condition; and the station has received much attention, with a platform being reinstated (left), buildings being renovated or rebuilt, signalling installed and trackwork improved. *John Hunt/John Stretton*

**PENRHYN: During the Ffestiniog's Centenary celebrations in 1963 crowds came to the railway in unprecedent-
ed numbers, but whether this is the cause of the traffic queue at Penrhyn crossing gates is uncertain! Everyone
seems relaxed, however, as *Merddin Emrys*, here still cableless and the mainstay of the line at this time, heads
north from the station on its way to Tan-y-Bwlch.**

By 7 June 1995 the road through Penrhyndeudraeth had improved, but happily there is a lack of traffic being

stuck at the crossing gates these days; regardless, *Merddin Emrys* is still plying northwards, but by now with much longer and heavier trains. The road has been resurfaced and yellow-lined, a bungalow has been built on the hillside and the trees have grown apace, obliterating the mountain in the background of the 1963 scene. The gentleman sitting on the wall, right, is Paul Davies, volunteer fireman on the FR and owner of the white house on the hill, which is still there, although also now hidden by those trees. *Jon Marsh/John Stretton*

TAN-Y-BWLCH was for many years the terminus of the railway, while efforts were being made to press on up the line. The station has seen some dramatic changes over the years, changing its previous unspoilt country ambience. Not everyone welcomed these developments, but it has to be said that they have been for the general benefit of passengers/visitors. In July 1965 *Linda* has just arrived from Portmadoc and the guard is in the process of unlocking the carriage doors in order that travellers can alight.

In 1968 an island platform was installed, at the time that the railway was extended to Ddualt, and the track was re-aligned at this time, as can be seen from this later view. Thirty years on, 7 June 1995, the first 'up' train of the day, the 0825 ex-Porthmadog, arrives at the station behind *Conway Castle*, halting at the side of the ex-1873 station building, now lovingly restored. On the extreme left is the brand new garden area, completed this year by the Buildings, Parks & Gardens Department volunteers. *Terry Gough/John Stretton*

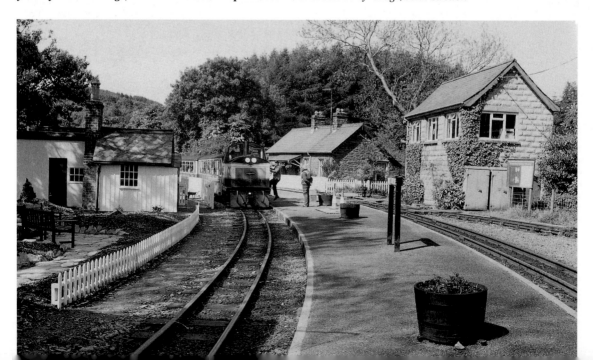

BLAENAU FFESTINIOG: Where the track splits is the site of the old FR Junction station (Stesion Fain), and the platform edging can just be seen to the left of the tracks. To the right is the old water tower; the ex-LMS station building, a 1956 rebuilding of the original after a fire, is to the left. The FR track was originally double throughout this area, continuing on between the buildings in the middle distance into the heart of the town, but by this time, 1969, rationalisation had taken place and the line had been severed by road developments some six years or so earlier.

This is obviously the same vantage point as so much remains, but on 6 June 1995 the ex-LMS station has been closed for 13 years and has suffered some vandalism, and the old Junction station wall has gone. The ex-FR track was taken up in the early 1970s and it was not until a decade later that the railway reappeared, this time travelling further to the right, under prestressed concrete bridges provided during the town by-pass development, to a new terminus beside the present-day BR station. *Hugh Tours, Martin Cook Collection/John Stretton*

DINAS JUNCTION, situated some 2½ miles south of Caernarvon, and closer to Llanwnda than Dinas, was less a junction than a meeting of two railways, the London & North Western branch from Bangor to Afonwen, and the North Wales Narrow Gauge/Welsh Highland Railway line to Portmadoc. Although undated, this view, showing the LNWR platforms and looking north towards Caernarvon, is conceivably in the station's last years, as apart from the signal box (which has lost its name from above the door), it is devoid of station furniture and the slate 'nameboard' is more than likely to be for the benefit of the photographer than any travelling passenger! The signal box is still open, however, with the occupant at the foot of the stairs and a clear signal at the far end of the platform, but there seems little prospect of any major traffic. Freight traffic was withdrawn from the LNWR branch on 4 May 1964, with passengers going with the closure of the route on the following 7 December. The Welsh Highland facilities, on the other side of the building on the right, were withdrawn at the close of September 1936 (passengers) and 1 June 1937 (goods and mineral traffic), but despite the passage of time the waiting room/booking office is still in good condition, which is more than can be said for the overgrown sloped entrance to the stations seen on the extreme right.

While it is still possible to stand on the same spot as the previous picture, the view is now blocked by a chain-link fence. Thus the June 1995 view is from a point roughly level with the end of the tree-lined entrance mentioned above, and the sloping roof of the ex-WHR booking office, still extant and in remarkably good condition, can just be seen to the extreme right. The platform edges of the standard gauge station form the edges of the current road and the car is at a point near to the old signal box. The joint FR/WHR plans for restoration of a railway between Caernarvon and Porthmadog will see tracks once more on this site, with Dinas Junction becoming the first goal as the new railway heads south. *Lens of Sutton/John Stretton*

SOUTH SNOWDON, more simply known as 'Snowdon' until October 1923, was situated on the WHR on the 'back-side' of the mountain, just short of a mile south from Llyn Cwellyn, on the road from Caernarvon to Porthmadog. This view, towards the mountain, was taken from the road in the late 1930s and shows the station after closure, but still somewhat incongruously attempting to charge 1 shilling for 'Parking Ground', a considerable sum for those days and roughly equivalent to £3 today!

Although not in exactly the same position as the earlier view, the present entrance to what is now a car park (and free at that!) bears an uncanny resemblance to the angle of the stone wall of the parking area in 1939, and even the new toilet block has been tastefully built to blend in with the surroundings. The evidence of rampant spread of undergrowth since the years of operation and closure, common to much of the ex-WHR route, is well seen in this June 1995 view. *WHS collection/John Stretton*

BEDDGELERT: A 1936 scene full of interest. Hunslet 2-6-2T No 901 *Russell* of 1906 slows for the station with a train from Dinas, as families prepare themselves both within and beside the rather less than glamorous corrugated iron building. This train terminates here and the passengers shown will enjoy the trip back up the line behind a bunker-first *Russell*; those passengers going down to Portmadoc will change here and travel in the train (unseen) to the right of *Russell*, behind Baldwin No 590, which can be seen running around its train. To the left of 590 a coalman and his mate attend to their load on the Model T lorry and the whole scene is one of bustle.

The contrast 30 years later could hardly be more dramatic. There is no bustle now, only the occasional human entry to disturb the birdsong and wildlife, and all that remains of the station is the concrete base, seen middle left among the grass clumps. The line curved from this point to the right, into a cutting to the right of the white house, and No 590 in the previous view stood just in front of that house. *Hugh Tours, Martin Cook collection/John Stretton*

Past and Present Colour The East Midlands

Leicestershire

LEICESTER LONDON ROAD (1) The north end of the station on Thursday 11 May 1967, with Class '25' diesel No D7581 (25231) awaiting departure on a parcels working. Entering the station on a St Pancras train is Class '45' No D90 (45008). The '25' was withdrawn on 23 August 1985 and returned to Leicester for scrapping at Vic Berry's yard, while D90 was withdrawn in December 1980 and languished at Swindon Works until cutting up took place in December 1983.

On Saturday 8 July 1995 the 11.00 to St Pancras enters the station with HST Class '43' power car No 43053 *Leeds United* leading. *Both Chris Banks*

LEICESTER LONDON ROAD (2): The north end again, but this time looking in the opposite direction into the station and showing the old Midland Railway buildings and overall roof. The date is again 11 May 1967 and Class '45' No D49 *The Manchester Regiment* (45039) prepares to leave on a mid-morning St Pancras to Sheffield express. This was another locomotive withdrawn in December 1980 and cut up at Swindon, this time in April 1983.

The same location on 8 July 1995 with the old station now rebuilt. Class '43' HST power car No 43083 has its windows cleaned by its driver while working a St Pancras to Sheffield service, departing from Leicester at 11.18. Both *Chris Bank*

LEICESTER MIDLAND SHED YARD in 1962, with visiting March-based 'B1' 4-6-0 No 61375 under the coaling tower. Withdrawal for this locomotive came on 25 November 1963, followed by a period of stationary boiler duty at Kings Lynn.

On 8 July 1995 the yard is seen from the same viewing point, the 'Birdcage' pathway. Visible are diesels Nos 60040 *Brecon Beacons*, 60077 *Canisp*, 56093 *The Institution of Mining Engineers* and 58036. *D. W. Webb, Colour-Rail/Chris Banks*

FOREST ROAD CROSSING, LEICESTER was situated on the line out from Belgrave Road station. In August 1960 'B1' 4-6-0 No 61177 heads a Saturdays-only Summer Season service for Skegness. The Midland line into Leicester London Road passes overhead.

At the same location on 9 September 1995 the track has gone and the level crossing erased. Nowadays it is impossible to stand in exactly the same spot as the earlier photographer, as this is now occupied by a warehouse. *D. W. Webb, Colour-Rail/Chris Banks*

Northamptonshire

KETTERING ENGINE SHED YARD in August 1962. Franco-Crosti-boilered '9F' 2-10-0 No 92029, a Kettering engine at the time and remarkably clean after a works visit, prepares for work after being turned on the turntable just visible in the background. Two months later the engine was transferred to Saltley, and finally ended its days at Birkenhead in November 1967.

Being situated adjacent to Kettering station, after closure on 14 June 1965 and demolition of the buildings, the shed site formed a useful area for the station car park. This was the view from the same position on Thursday 1 June 1995. *D. F. Cole, Colour-Rail/Chris Banks*

WELLINGBOROUGH, looking north from the overbridge near the station in July 1955. Kentish Town-based Stanier '5MT' 4-6-0 No 44825 heads back to its base with an express from Nottingham. Wellingborough shed is over to the right. No 44825 was withdrawn from Carlisle Kingmoor during the week ended 7 October 1967.

The same location on Sunday 21 May 1989 sees HST power car No 43048 bringing up the rear of a St Pancras to Sheffield working. Wellingborough No 2 roundhouse still stands and is nowadays used as an industrial unit. *Chris Banks collection/Chris Banks*

Cambridgeshire

PETERBOROUGH station, north end: in September 1958 'A2/2' 4-6-2 No 60504 *Mons Meg* runs in light engine for an engine change. This was a New England engine, and had been transferred to the shed from Edinburgh Haymarket during the week ended 14 January 1950. It remained at Peterborough until withdrawal on 23 January 1961.

The buildings in the background are the link in this view of Class 153 single unit DMU No 153384 arriving at the rebuilt and remodelled Peterborough station to form the 16.09 to Gainsborough. The date is Saturday 22 July 1995.
D. Smith, Colour-Rail/Chris Banks

CAMBRIDGE: A sunny day in 1959 finds 'B2' 4-6-0 No 61644 *Earlham Hall* leaving Cambridge station with a King's Cross train. The 'B2' was a Thompson two-cylinder rebuild from a 'B17' with a 100A boiler; this example was withdrawn from March shed later that same year, on 25 November.

On Wednesday 10 May 1989 EMU No 317372, forming the 10.20 to King's Cross, leaves the now electrified station. *D. M. C. Hepburne-Scott, Colour-Rail/Chris Banks*

North West, West and South West London

CAMDEN BANK: Before the practice of utilising carriage cleaners at stations rather than at carriage depots came into being, to avoid the majority of empty coaching stock workings from main-line termini, Fowler '3MT' Class 2-6-2T No 40053 hauls the stock of an earlier main-line arrival at Euston up Camden Bank to Willesden for attention on 3 October 1959.

Currently, empty stock workings are minimal and, for the most part, are restricted to sleeper services. At the same location, just over halfway up Camden Bank, on 27 June 1995, are two Class '321/4' EMUs, Nos 321408 and 321422, the former completing its journey from Northampton to Euston and the latter beginning its journey to Birmingham New Street. Most of the background buildings remain, but a number are now obscured by much thicker tree growth. *R. C. Riley/Brian Morrison*

NORTH POLE JUNCTION: Passing the 1922 LNWR North Pole Junction signal box on 8 August 1959, Collett '5700' Class 0-6-0 Pannier tank No 8756 heads for Southern Region metals with a freight from Acton. Since the 'present' view at this location in the black & white section of *BR Past and Present No 13* was taken in April 1989 (page 35), the signal box has been demolished and all the trappings of overhead electrification are evident for the use of Channel Tunnel 'Eurostar' trains. On 7 June 1995 Class '60' No 60018 *Moel Siabod* is seen hauling a 'Yeoman' stone train from Merehead to Crawley. *R. C. Riley/Ken Brunt*

KENSINGTON OLYMPIA: Elegant Marsh 'H2' Class 'Atlantic' No 32424 *Beachy Head* blows off steam leaving Kensington Olympia on 18 August 1956, hauling a summer-only cross-country train from Hastings to Leicester.

A tall wire fence now prevents quite the same angle being taken today, as Brush Class '60' No 60043 *Yes Tor* passes the same place with a 'MainLine Freight Ltd' train of Tiphook wagons heading for the ex-GWR main line. The junction from the old transit shed has been taken out, and unsightly electrical boxes have appeared where the semaphore signal once stood. The road bridge is still in situ and in the interim has been painted green and yellow. *R. C. Riley/Ken Brunt*

CLAPHAM CUTTING: On the Central Section tracks through Clapham Cutting, Fairburn '4MT' Class 2-6-4T No 42106 passes with the 16.08 Victoria-Tunbridge Wells West train on 20 June 1959.

The location today has changed very little, although the trees have grown a little taller, the embankment walls are blackened and tower blocks have appeared on the horizon. A large bush now grows where the once blackened grass was apparent. On 7 June 1995 Class '423/1' 4VEP No 3435 leads the 10.24 train from Victoria to East Grinstead. *R. C. Riley/Brian Morrison*

NINE ELMS SHED: Outside the London end of 70A on 6 September 1958, Maunsell 'S15' Class 4-6-0 No 30839 is watered before departing for Waterloo to take out its train, while rebuilt Bulleid 'Merchant Navy' 'Pacific' No 35012 *United States Line* arrives on depot to replenish its tender before making the same journey back to the terminus.

Nothing whatever remains of the once large Nine Elms Shed complex, and the same view today is the grassy perimeter of the New Covent Garden Market. The balconied flats in the background remain as a reference. *R. C. Riley/Ken Brunt*

SOUTHALL (1): Approaching Southall with the 13.30 Paddington-Penzance 'Royal Duchy' express on 10 August 1957, Collett 'King' Class 4-6-0 No 6004 *King George III* passes Southall engine shed; the headboard displays the arms of the Duchy of Cornwall.

In the same position on 7 June 1995 InterCity Class '47/4' No 47847 hurries by with the 14.18 Paddington-Edinburgh 'Midland Scot'. Trackwork has been reduced, the land containing the sidings in the background has been sold off - and the almost mandatory 'Virol' advertisement of the day has of course been removed. *R. C. Riley/Brian Morrison*

SOUTHALL (2): Looking in the opposite direction at Southall on the same August day in 1957, the 08.30 Plymouth-Paddington 'Mayflower' express is powered through the station by 'King' Class 4-6-0 No 6027 *King Richard I.*

Although the background water tower and gasholder buildings remain, the changes that have occurred at this scene are myriad. Passing through the platforms on 7 June 1995, Class 166 'Turbo Expresses' Nos 166210 leading 166221 form a train from Oxford to Paddington. *R. C. Riley/Brian Morrison*

BEACONSFIELD: Grime-encrusted 'King' 4-6-0 No 6011 *King James I* approaches Beaconsfield on 4 August 1962, hauling the well-known 14.10 Paddington-Birkenhead express.

On 3 July 1995 the lineside telegraph poles have gone, but the old wooden paling fence survives, as does the footbridge. This, however, is now obscured by the very large bush that 33 years before was quite a small bush. Class '165/0' 'Chiltern Turbo' No 165039 passes forming the 15.10 service from Marylebone to High Wycombe. *R. C. Riley/Ken Brunt*

Past and Present Colour

Avon, Cotswolds and the Malverns

HENWICK: On 9 September 1961 'Castle' No 7027 _Thornbury Castle_ accelerates from Henwick with the 12.45 pm Paddington to Hereford express. The station and closing level crossing gates can clearly be seen in the background, as can the city of Worcester on the horizon. Until closure in 1965, Henwick was the first station west of Worcester.

Today all trace of the station has gone, although the signal box and level crossing remain. Most services between Worcester and Hereford are operated by Regional Railways, with a much-reduced InterCity service to Paddington. On 10 March 1995 Class '150' No 150128 heads west with the 11.31 Birmingham New Street to Hereford via Kidderminster service. _Michael Mensing/John Whitehouse_

ASHCHURCH: Activity at Ashchurch on 15 June 1963 as a Swindon-built Cross Country DMU approaches on the main line while Pannier tank 0-6-0 No 3745 stands at the head of the 10.00 am Evesham train; this was the last day of the branch-line service. The main-line station, clearly visible in the background, remained open until 1971.

There remains today a short spur off the main line, serving the nearby MOD depot. Little is left of the station except part of the old branch-line platform, which can be seen in this January 1995 view. The Class '158' 'Express' unit is working a Nottingham to Cardiff service. Recently plans have been announced to reopen Ashchurch station.
Hugh Ballantyne/Geoff Dowling

GLOUCESTER EASTGATE: On 8 September 1962 two southbound summer trains stand side by side at Gloucester Eastgate. 'Royal Scot' 4-6-0 No 46112 *Sherwood Forester* has the road while Stanier Class '5' 4-6-0 No 44816 awaits a path. Note the extensive sidings on the right. Behind the photographer is Barton Road level crossing; the road congestion caused by this and others nearby was a major reason for Eastgate's closure in 1975.

Redevelopment has totally obliterated any trace of the railway, with only local landmarks to identify the spot. A supermarket now occupies the site of Eastgate, with part of the trackbed being taken over by Gloucester's inner ring road. *Alan Jarvis/John Whitehouse*

COALEY JUNCTION: 'Jubilee' 4-6-0 No 45725 *Repulse* is seen on 7 July 1962 heading a northbound express through Coaley Junction. Note the station and junction signal box in the background, with the branch to Cam and Dursley diverging to the left. The station closed in 1965.

A new station opened near to the site of the old junction station in 1994, taking the name of Cam & Dursley. Up-to-date facilities are provided including a footbridge with ramps to facilitate ease of access for the disabled and the now usual basic waiting shelter. The passage of a northbound IC125 seems to have caused some local excitement. *Michael Mensing/Geoff Dowling*

STONEHOUSE: An early 1960s scene at Stonehouse, Burdett Road, on the Great Western route from Gloucester to Swindon, as an auto-train awaits departure with ex-GWR 0-4-2T No 1453 in charge. Note the impressive station building, of Brunel design. Stonehouse also had a station on the Midland line from Gloucester to Bristol, which closed in 1965.

The scene today reveals the rationalisation that has taken place, with the brick-built waiting shelter now providing customer comfort. On 13 March 1995 'Sprinter' No 150248 approaches with the 13.22 Gloucester to Swindon service. *John Dew/Geoff Dowling*

BRIMSCOMBE: Another 0-4-2T, No 1409, restarts a local auto-train working from Brimscombe on 5 June 1962. The service is probably a Stroud-Chalford train, consisting of just one coach. To the rear of the train can be seen a couple of wagons in the station goods yard.

The station closed in 1964, with now only a foot crossing to mark the location. In the background can be seen The King & Castle public house, commemorating the famous GWR express passenger locomotive classes. Today's high-speed express is represented by Class '43' No 43172 leading a Paddington-bound InterCity 125. *Alan Jarvis/Geoff Dowling*

LYDNEY TOWN: On 29 October 1970 a Class '22' diesel-hydraulic locomotive leads a ballast train from Whitecliffe Quarry through Lydney Town. The crossing gates protect the A48 Chepstow-Gloucester main road.

The line has now been reopened by the Dean Forest Railway, who operate trains between Lydney Junction (near the BR station) and Norchard. On 1 May 1994 0-6-0PT No 9681 approaches the level crossing with a passenger train. The platform facing of the old Town station can clearly be seen on the right. *Both W. Potter*

SOUDLEY: A classic Forest of Dean scene, as Pannier tank 0-6-0 No 3675 passes Soudley with a rake of coal empties on 11 October 1965. Note the fireman who is chalking the cab number plate for the benefit of the photographer. The scene today has changed little, except for the removal of the railway. *Both W. Potter*

Nottinghamshire and Derbyshire

DERBY station, platform 1, in May 1964, with immaculate Stanier '5MT' 4-6-0 No 44918 with the empty coach stock of the Royal Train. The engine is in the later unlined livery after a visit to Crewe Works the previous month. It had also been built at Crewe and entered traffic in December 1945 at Leicester Midland depot. Withdrawal came from Trafford Park in January 1967.

Arriving at platform 1 on Sunday 16 July 1995 is Class '43' HST power car No 43058 on the 09.15 St Pancras to Sheffield. Much remains the same, except for the original station buildings now replaced by a more modern design. *Colour-Rail/Chris Banks*

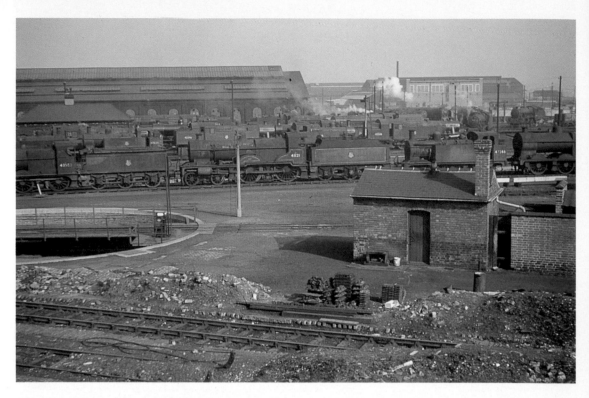

DERBY LOCOMOTIVE SHED YARD in March 1960. This is the view from London Road bridge, which for decades was a favourite place for train-spotters. Centre stage is '4P' Compound 4-4-0 No 41121, which had been in store since withdrawal from the Derby allocation in February 1959. Derby shed closed to steam in March 1967.

The view from London Road bridge on Sunday 16 July 1995 shows only parcels vans Nos 92978 and 92979 to look at. After closure the shed buildings remained in use until demolition in 1969. Over to the left is the Derby power signal box. *F. Hornby, Colour-Rail/Chris Banks*

DUFFIELD (1) is 5 miles north of Derby on the Midland main line, and marks the beginnings of the Peak District hills. Passing St Alkmund's church, half a mile south of Duffield station, is Class '45' No D48 (45038) on what is thought to be the late-running northbound 'Devonian' on Saturday 30 April 1966. The locomotive was withdrawn in June 1985 from Toton depot and cut up at Vic Berry's Leicester yard in October 1986.

The same view from the stone overbridge on Saturday 23 September 1995, as HST power car No 43059 heads north on a St Pancras to Sheffield working. The rationalisation of the track is apparent, as is the growth of lineside foliage, making photography difficult due to the strong shadows. *Michael Mensing/Chris Banks*

DUFFIELD (2): The view north at Duffield from the footbridge seen in the previous photographs. Birkenhead-based Standard '9F' 2-10-0 No 92011 rolls past with southbound empties on Saturday 30 April 1966. This engine had spent most of its existence allocated to Annesley working the fast freight services on the Great Central to Woodford Halse. Withdrawal came in November 1967.

On Saturday 23 September 1995 a Freightliner for Bescot passes the same spot hauled by two Tinsley-based Class '47s', Nos 47297 (D1999) and 47306 *The Sapper* (D1787). *Michael Mensing/Chris Banks*

AMBERGATE JUNCTION on the same afternoon, Saturday 30 April 1966. Green-liveried Class '47' No D1799 (47318) comes off the Sheffield line with an up freight. The line to Matlock and through the Peak to Manchester curves away to the left.

Twenty-two years later, on Sunday 22nd May 1988, an unidentified Class '47' comes off the Sheffield line with a Bristol-bound express. The line to Manchester is no more, being now only a branch to Matlock. *Michael Mensing/Chris Banks*

BUXTON MIDLAND station in August 1962. This station was opened on 1 June 1863 and situated parallel to the LNWR station, separated by the station forecourt. As can be seen, it comprised only a single track with platforms on both sides. LMS '4F' 0-6-0 No 44080, allocated to Rowsley shed, stands in the morning sun awaiting departure with the single coach for Millers Dale to connect with the main line trains to Manchester. No 44080 was withdrawn in July 1964 from Coalville shed.

The Midland station closed on 6 March 1967 and today no trace survives; the site is now part of the car park and road. The ex-LNWR station remains in use, as seen in this view recorded on 16 July 1995. *The late B. Metcalf, Colour-Rail/Chris Banks*

BUXTON STEAM DEPOT in May 1953. This was an LNWR-built, six-road straight shed opened in 1892, and situated alongside the Buxton to Stockport line. It remained open until 4 March 1968 and its last allocation of Stanier '8F' 2-8-0s was transferred to the remaining steam sheds in Manchester.

The depot site is seen in the second view dated Sunday 16 July 1995. The link with the earlier photograph is the line of trees on the hillside in the background. *J. H. Moss, Colour-Rail/Chris Banks*

LENTON SOUTH JUNCTION, west of Nottingham Midland station, in May 1965, with an unusual visitor in the shape of 'O4/8' Class 2-8-0 No 63639 on an eastbound freight. The line curving away to the left is to Radford and Basford Vernon. The 2-8-0 was withdrawn from Colwick shed in December of the same year.

On Saturday 23 September 1995 the junction is controlled from a distant power box, the old Midland box gone. Class '150' DMU No 150132 approaches with the 11.05 Nottingham to Crewe working. *Chris Banks collection/Chris Banks*

Past and Present Colour

East Yorkshire

HULL, ALEXANDRA DOCK (1): From the end of steam until its closure in 1982 diesel shunters were employed on Alexandra Dock. On Saturday 10 October 1964 examples of Classes '03', '08' and '11' are lined up waiting for duty on Monday morning. Note the pointed roof of Hull prison above the fourth engine.

Although Alexandra Dock was re-opened to shipping in 1991, it was unfortunately not re-connected to the railway system. However, the original buildings and tower, and even the telegraph post on the left, remain in the summer of 1994. The tower (which is a listed structure) is technically an Hydraulic Accumulator Tower, containing a large pig-iron press that would force a head of water under pressure through an internal pipe system to operate hydraulic capstans, lock gates, etc. *D. J. Mitchell/Carey Vessey*

HULL, ALEXANDRA DOCK (2): Another view of Alexandra Dock on 10 October 1964, during a rare visit by a passenger train, a railtour formed of a Birmingham DMU set. The tracks in the foreground gave access to the former H&B high-level goods lines. Note Alexandra Dock signal box and the wealth of detail and general air of activity compared with the modern view.

The only features remaining to connect the two pictures 30 years apart are the lamp standard on the right, the roadway and the Alexandra Dock shed tower on the left. The photographer's car is standing astride the remnants of the track at the site of the level crossing. Despite the absence of rail traffic, Alexandra Dock remains very busy today. *D. J. Mitchell/Carey Vessey*

HULL VICTORIA PIER: People who had bought a railway ticket at Hull Victoria Pier station would cross the road to the ramp leading to the rail-operated New Holland Ferry, as shown in this 1967 view.

The ferry service ceased on the opening of the Humber Bridge in June 1981 and the ramp was demolished, although the adjoining building remains. The classic lines of the Mark I Cortina contrast with the vehicle styles of 20-30 years later. *J. Spencer Gilks/Roger Hill*

HORNSEA BRIDGE: Freight traffic at Hornsea was handled in the low-level yard here. In this rare view taken on 10 October 1964 LMS Class '4' 2-6-0 No 43069 waits to depart for Hull with a load of mineral wagons. The line to Hornsea Bridge and Hornsea Town stations is on the embankment in the foreground.

The embankment is still in place in spring 1994 and the goods yard is being developed as a light industrial estate. The four rooftops in the centre of the picture identify the location. *D. J. Mitchell/Roger Hill*

STAMFORD BRIDGE: 'B1' No 61306 arrives at Stamford Bridge with the midday service from Hull to York on 27 November 1965, the last day of service on the York-Market Weighton-Beverley-Hull line. Even on this last day the station staff had been busy shovelling the snow.

By early 1994 the station buildings have been extended and converted into a youth centre, and the crossing-keeper's house has also acquired an extension. A great deal of effort has been made to preserve the railway atmosphere at Stamford Bridge, even to the extent of constructing a mock level crossing gate across the trackbed. *D. J. Mitchell/Roger Hill*

MARKET WEIGHTON: A York-Hull Cravens DMU arrives at Market Weighton on the morning of the same final day. Note the tail lamp on the front!

As mentioned elsewhere, it is very difficult 30 years later to find any trace whatsoever of the railway at Market Weighton. The railwaymen's cottages on the right do, however, remain, although because of the housing development that now covers the site, a slightly different viewpoint has had to be adopted. *D. J. Mitchell/Roger Hill*

KIPLING COTES station, between Market Weighton and Beverley, is host to a two-car Cravens DMU forming a Hull-York service in 1964; note the closure notice attached to the buffer-stop.

Apart from the use of the trackbed as the Hudsons Way footpath, little has changed at this remote location, and the restored station buildings and goods shed are now occupied by an antiques dealer. Even the signal box survives, immediately behind the photographer. *J. Spencer Gilks/Roger Hill*

HOLME MOOR: No 3442 *The Great Marquess* heads the 'Whitby Moors Rail Tour' through Holme Moor, between Selby and Market Weighton, on 6 March 1965. Like the line, which closed completely three months later, the signal box has begun to fall apart.

The photographer's wife Jean surveys the scene from the same goods dock in the spring of 1994. The trackbed is a footpath and one of the concrete crossing gate posts survives. *D. J. Mitchell/Roger Hill*

South Wales
Part 1

CALDICOT HALT, on the main line from Gloucester near Severn Tunnel Junction, was a typical example of a GWR standard timber halt, large numbers of which were built from 1903 onwards to serve remote country communities. The lineside platforms were designed to be constructed cheaply and comprised a series of rectangular timber frames on which the platform, made up of planks, was laid. The corrugated iron 'Pagoda' shelter was another standard GWR architectural feature. Opened on 12 September 1932, Caldicot Halt survived the mass closures of the 1960s and continued to be served by the local trains that worked between Gloucester and Cardiff. Our April 1961 illustration shows the original timber-built Halt with an ex-GWR '2800' Class locomotive passing with a Gloucester-bound freight.

A visit to Caldicot on Friday 14 April 1995 was timed to record the arrival of Class 158 'Express' unit No 158 833 with the 0735 Milford Haven to Birmingham New Street. There is no timber or corrugated iron in the replacement structure now provided at Caldicot, with up-to-date style paved platforms and glazed shelters. *Alan Jarvis/Don Gatehouse*

NEWPORT HIGH STREET: A through passenger service off the Southern Region provides the subject of our view of Newport station on 23 March 1963, with '4900' 'Hall' Class No 6929 *Whorlton Hall* providing the customary motive power for such inter-regional passenger workings. On the right a '2800' Class locomotive approaches on the down through line with a westbound freight.

Class 158 'Express' units were introduced in South Wales in May 1991 and now provide the staple train formation on services to and from the South Coast of England. The corresponding view taken on Saturday 27 August 1994 shows No 158 818 setting off on the final leg of its journey to Cardiff Central with the 1024 from Portsmouth Harbour. *Alan Jarvis/Don Gatehouse*

PONTLLANFRAITH (LOW LEVEL) (1): Situated on the former Taff Vale Extension line that linked Pontypool Road with the Vale of Neath, Pontllanfraith saw considerable freight traffic during the steam era. On 27 July 1963 one of the versatile Churchward '4300' Class 2-6-0 mixed traffic locomotives, No 6361, approaches from Crumlin with a train of mineral wagons. This particular Churchward locomotive was one of a batch built at Swindon in 1923 and as such was not fitted with outside steam pipes and the side-window cab that was a feature of the later Collett-produced variants.

With the passage of nearly 32 years the corresponding view shows that part of the site is now used as a parking area for the nearby parish church. The recess in the embankment where the signal box stood can still be located amongst the undergrowth, and the track alignment to the left of the Church Hall is also visible. *Alan Jarvis/Geoff Dowling*

PONTLLANFRAITH (LOW LEVEL) (2): Our second illustration at this location on 27 July 1963 shows '5600' Class 0-6-2T No 5647 entering with a passenger service *en route* to Pontypool Road. Above the coaches of the train can be seen the back of the all-timber structure of Pontllanfraith High Level Station signal box, which controlled the level crossing situated at the southern end of the platforms. The road bridge that gave access to the railway crossing is visible to the rear of the train, and just beyond the road bridge is the railway bridge that took the Sirhowy Valley line over the Taff Vale Extension route.

The April 1995 view of the same location confirms the total transformation of the former railway alignment, with no visible trace of either the station, bridges or level crossing remaining. *Alan Jarvis/Geoff Dowling*

QUAKER'S YARD (HIGH LEVEL): On a sunny 31 March 1962 '5700' Class 0-6-0PT No 3685 arrives at Quaker's Yard (High Level) station with the late morning service from Aberdare (High Level) to Pontypool Road. The train was scheduled to cover the 23 miles in 67 minutes with 11 intermediate stops. At Quaker's Yard passengers from Merthyr Tydfil could connect with this service via the adjacent Low Level station.

The route across from Pontypool Road closed in June 1964 and our view of the same location exactly 30 years later shows no trace of the former railway, the land having been sold and redeveloped for private housing. Even the colliery spoil tips that once featured in the distance have been re-profiled to provide a more natural contour to the background hills. *Alan Jarvis/Don Gatehouse*

CRUMLIN (LOW LEVEL): A tramroad linking Beaufort Ironworks with the canal at Crumlin was opened in 1796, and some 60 years later it was converted to a standard gauge railway. With the original ironworks closed and superseded by steel production plants, imported iron ore had to be transported from Newport Docks up the Ebbw Valley for many decades. In 1954 the first of the British Railways Standard '9F' 2-10-0 locomotives were allocated to Newport Ebbw Junction specifically for this arduous work. It is therefore appropriate to illustrate both Crumlin and a train loaded with iron ore *en route* to Ebbw Vale Steelworks being banked by a BR '9F' in this view taken on 27 July 1963. Two of the slender pillars of Crumlin viaduct, which carried the Pontypool to Neath line 200 feet above the track level of the Western Valleys route, are also visible in the photograph.

With the establishment of steel plants on the coastal plain, the British Steel Corporation ceased production at Ebbw Vale, which then concentrated on the specialist work of producing tin plate and galvanised steel. Our view of the location in 1995 shows a trainload of steel coil from Llanwern heading up the valley in the care of Class 60 No 60093 *Jack Stirk*. *Alan Jarvis/Geoff Dowling*

LLANHILLETH: Viewed on 31 July 1963 from the road that follows the east side of the valley, the extent of the railway infrastructure that once served the Ebbw Vale is clearly illustrated. Above the short freight that is heading down the valley is Llanhilleth Steam Coal Colliery, and to the left can be seen Llanhilleth Branch Junction Middle Signal Box. The two tracks on the right lead to the single line that climbs up to join the Pontypool Road to Neath route at Crumlin Junction.

Unfortunately, the level of tree growth that had taken place in the intervening years prevented access for an exactly corresponding view, but the extent of the changes is all too evident when you compare the above illustration from the steam era with the March 1995 version. The elevated section of the A467 expressway overshadows the much rationalised railway, where Class 60 No 60033 *Samuel Johnson* is visible slowly threading its way up the valley with another consignment of steel coil for Ebbw Vale. *Alan Jarvis & Don Gatehouse*

PONTLLANFRAITH (HIGH LEVEL): With the conversion from tramroad to railway completed in the 1860s to make an end-on connection with the Monmouthshire Railway at Nine Mile Point, a passenger service via Risca to Newport Dock Street commenced on 19 June 1865. Unfortunately, the passenger services over the former Sirhowy Valley line did not survive to celebrate their centenary and had ceased in June 1960. However, sections of the route continued to be used by what little freight traffic remained for a number of years thereafter, until the cessation of freight operations between Risca and Tredegar in May 1970. On 27 July 1963 a '5700' Class locomotive stands on the former up line at the north end of the then closed Pontllanfraith High Level station with a local freight working. Note that the tracks of the former down line in the foreground have been removed and weeds grow unchecked on the platforms.

Since the closure of the line local road developments have obliterated almost all trace of the former railway. However, our corresponding view taken in April 1995 shows the survival of a section of the old platform face beneath the trees that have now matured to shade the remains of the station site. *Alan Jarvis/ Geoff Dowling*

Past and Present Colour

Lincolnshire

NEW HOLLAND PIER: 'Britannia' 'Pacific' No 70040 *Clive of India* backs the stock of the 14.27 Skegness-New Holland Pier off the pier on 24 August 1963. The train is partly formed of non-corridor suburban stock and the engine will turn on the triangle to the south of New Holland Town station.

The pier, track, buildings and signal box survive in the ownership of New Holland Bulk Services Limited, to whom thanks are due for allowing access. The track on which the 'Britannia' was running is intact beneath the conveyor. *R. E. Burdon/Carey Vessey*

SAXILBY is on the former Great Northern & Great Eastern Joint line between Gainsborough and Lincoln. On 26 January 1963 'WD' 2-8-0 No 90545 leaves with a pick-up freight for Lincoln.

The same location in February 1995 sees a Class 153 single-car unit forming a Doncaster-Lincoln service. The station is still open and the buildings remain behind the train, although housing (appropriately known as The Sidings) covers the former goods yard. *R. E. Burdon/Roger Hill*

WADDINGTON was on the former Great Northern line between Lincoln and Honington Junction near Grantham, which was frequently used by East Coast trains diverted from the main line. Here a typically grimy York 'A1' 'Pacific', No 60140 *Balmoral*, heads south with a diverted express on 16 April 1961.

The line closed completely on 1 November 1965 and a house now occupies the station site, although the former station house remains on the right. *R. E. Burdon/Roger Hill*

HARMSTON is a few miles south of Waddington on the Lincoln-Honington Junction line, and on 16 April 1961 the immortal *Mallard* approaches the station with another up East Coast diversion.

The authors claim a 'first' for this series with the first picture of *Mallard* running in service on a line that no longer exists! The second picture shows the abandoned trackbed at the same location in March 1995; note the same pattern of the trees in the right background. *R. E. Burdon/Roger Hill*

WOODHALL JUNCTION is on the former Lincoln-Boston line; here a two-car Cravens DMU set forms a Lincoln-Skegness service on 2 May 1970. This was the junction for the line to Woodhall Spa and Horncastle.

In common with most of the lines in East Lincolnshire, this section of the Lincoln-Boston line perished in October 1970, but the station buildings and platforms survive in April 1995. *J. Spencer Gilks/Roger Hill*

MABLETHORPE on 3 August 1963, with LMS 'Crab' 2-6-0 No 42855 leaving with the summer Saturday 11.24 to Radford (Nottingham). This train ran via Firsby, Stickney, the Lincoln Avoiding Line and the Lancashire, Derbyshire & East Coast line to Shirebrook, Mansfield Midland and Radford. Note the typical practice of the day of cultivating the land right up to the trackside - the 'Crab' is picking its way through potatoes, green beans and rhubarb.

The Mablethorpe branch closed in October 1970 and the trackbed at this point is now occupied by the home of Mr & Mrs B. Krajnyak who kindly allowed access to their back garden for this picture to be taken. The building on the right provides the obvious connection. *R. E. Burdon/Roger Hill*

FIRSBY is seen here in August 1969, a little over a year before complete closure; a Sulzer Type 2 diesel comes off the Skegness line into the station with a train for Bradford, as a DMU awaits entry in the background to form either a Lincoln or Mablethorpe service. Note the wealth of detail in the crossing gates and signalling.

All that remains at Firsby in April 1995 are a couple of the station houses, the end of the down platform (just visible under the window of the gatehouse on the right) and the goods shed (behind the photographer). Another link with the past is former Firsby railwayman John Thornley, now Station Foreman at Skegness, who kindly allowed access to his garden (the former trackbed) for this picture to be taken.
J. Spencer Gilks/Roger Hill

SIBSEY is on the former East Lincolnshire main line between Boston and Firsby. Class 31 diesel No D5835 heads south with a Skegness-Leeds train on 12 August 1972.

The line from Boston is now single as far as Sibsey and becomes double from just north of the Great Northern signal box to Skegness. In April 1995 the Sibsey signalman opens the crossing gates by hand prior to the passage of a Coventry-Skegness 'Sprinter' - this is a delightfully quaint practice still to be found at several remote outposts in Lincolnshire, and a refreshing change from the normal blaring sirens and flashing lights. *J. Spencer Gilks/Roger Hill*

Past and Present Colour

The Tarka Trail

A line for all seasons - this first pair of photographs does not show change across the years, but just from season to season in this most beautiful part of England. The first shows the 'Tarka Line' in the summer of 1994; Class '150' No 150219 is seen near Portsmouth Arms on a Barnstaple-bound train.

The same location in winter is in some ways more attractive and gives an indication of the beauty to be seen outside the holiday season. Class '153' No 153382 is heading for Exeter. *Terry Gough/Stuart Smallridge*

An up train approaches King's Nympton on 28 July 1963. This is the 09.55 Ilfracombe to Waterloo service hauled by 'Battle of Britain' Class No 34072 *257 Squadron*. The wooden signal guarding the down line is a survivor of the LSWR; by this time almost all others had been replaced by iron lattice or rail-built posts with metal arms. The bridge in the background carries the Exeter Road to Barnstaple.

September 1994 finds both the railway and the road downgraded. The 'Tarka Line' is now a branch rather than a main line and the Exeter Road has lost its importance following the building of the North Devon Link Road from the M5 motorway to Barnstaple. The train is the 10.10 from Barnstaple to Exmouth consisting of Class '150' No **150238**. *Lawrence Golden/Terry Gough*

Barnstaple Junction during the diesel locomotive era finds Class '22' No D6313 outside the goods shed on 8 June 1967. The main station buildings are beyond the shed and the island platform is to the left, just out of view.

The present-day trains seem dwarfed by the platform built to accommodate the long London-bound services. The goods yard has been cleared and the view of the houses in the background is partly obscured by new buildings. The goods shed is isolated from the railway and has taken on a distinct lean to the right. *Frank Hornby/Terry Gough*

Barnstaple Town station long after the last train had departed. It was expected that the station would be demolished as the track and signalling had already been removed. The building itself was clearly in a poor state of repair.

However, the area subsequently sprang to life. The present view, while very different, clearly shows that a railway once passed here. The station buildings and the signal box have been retained, although surrounded by houses. The station buildings were used as a restaurant until 1994, but are currently unoccupied. *Both Terry Gough*

The long climb out of Ilfracombe gave rise to spectacular sights in the days of heavy steam-hauled trains. On 27 July 1963 'Battle of Britain' Class No 34079 *141 Squadron* pilots Class '4300' No 7333 on an evening train to Taunton.

The embankment along this stretch of line is now overgrown, although the foot and cycle path gives an opportunity to follow the course of the railway. Identifying particular spots is difficult, but the unusual bare tree in the centre background eliminated any doubt when it came to this one. *Lawrence Golden/Terry Gough*

A special train masquerading as the 'Atlantic Coast Express' passes Instow on 2 April 1978 hauled by Class '33' No 33105 on a tour from Waterloo to Meldon and Meeth.

Although Instow is closed there is much evidence of the railway with the restored signal box, most of the station and even some track. This is the same location in September 1994 showing the trackbed in its new guise as the Tarka Trail. *Spencer Taylor/Terry Gough*

Class '25' No 25170 leaves Torrington for Barnstaple with clay from Meeth and Marland clay works in October 1977. The main station platform and building is to the right, although little remains of the platform on the other side.

Cyclists now use the Tarka Trail where trains once passed. The station building is now a public house giving a sound excuse to rest before continuing one's journey. *Spencer Taylor/Terry Gough*

Watergate Halt was in most attractive surroundings and was well worth a visit, whether or not to catch one of the very infrequent trains. This is the halt in June 1967.

Watergate forms part of today's Tarka Trail. Some visitors make a point of cycling along the platform, an activity not permitted at stations still in use! *Frank Hornby/Terry Gough*

LINCOLNSHIRE

Roger Hill and Carey Vessey

WINTERTON & THEALBY was on the northern section of the Scunthorpe-Whitton North Lindsey Light Railway, built by the Great Central and opened in 1906. Passenger services on the line ceased as early as 1925, and by 1967 the sole user of the northern section was the British Steel Corporation, which purchased it from BR. It continued to be used by ironstone traffic until the closure of Thealby mine in 1980, and was then abandoned. The southern section of the line from Scunthorpe to Normanby Park and Flixborough Wharf still remains in BR ownership and use, and is covered in the Lincolnshire 'Past and Present' volume (No 27). In the 'past' picture, dating from September 1962, ironstone for the Scunthorpe blast furnaces of Richard Thomas & Baldwin's Redbourne Works heads south through the station behind one of their North British diesel-hydraulic 0-6-0s, which were new in 1957. Locomotives belonging to British Steel and its subsidiaries were a common sight on the branch for many years.

By June 1995 the trackbed has been converted into a private roadway used by lorries carrying waste to a landfill site near Roxby. *John Foreman/Roger Hill*

CLEETHORPES: 'Britannia' 'Pacific' No 70012 *John of Gaunt* takes advantage of the Cleethorpes turntable on 2 October 1965 while working an RCTS railtour from Nottingham. Steam-hauled passenger services in the area had ceased by this date and this was probably the last occasion that the turntable was used to turn a steam locomotive.

The site can be readily identified today, although Cleethorpes is now served only by 'Sprinters' and Class 153 single units, so the track in the foreground is redundant. The 'main' line passes behind the new building on the left. *John Foreman/Roger Hill*

LINCOLN (1): The former Great Northern shed at Lincoln (coded 40A), with ex-Great Central 'A5' 'Pacific' tank No 69820 prominent, on 10 April 1960.

The shed closed in January 1964, but amazingly, more than 30 years later, the buildings survive virtually intact. There is a rumour that the main shed building is to be converted into a facility for the new University proposed to be built on the surrounding land, although a lot of work will first have to be done on the potentially dangerous asbestos roof. *R. E. Burdon/Carey Vessey*

**LINCOLN (2): A delightful view of light 'O2/1' No 63923 ambling west past Spa Street, Lincoln, in 1951.
The Lincoln-Market Rasen-Barnetby line survives today, and in April 1995 a Class 153 forming a Grimsby-Lincoln service passes the same terraced housing.**
G. Clarke/Roger Hill

BARDNEY was the junction on the former Great Northern Lincoln-Boston line for the branch across the Wolds to Louth. On 16 May 1954 ex-GN 'J6' 0-6-0 No 64199 waits to leave with the RCTS Lincolnshire railtour, bound for Louth, Willoughby (via Mablethorpe), Firsby, Spilsby, Woodhall Junction, Horncastle and Lincoln.

The Lincoln-Boston line closed in 1970, although a freight facility to Bardney continued until 1983 to serve the adjoining British Sugar Corporation works. The present view (with the BSC works prominent) was taken in June 1993 when the up platform and buildings were still intact; they have since been demolished. *Hugh Ballantyne/Roger Hill*

WRAGBY station on the Bardney to Louth branch sees 'J6' No 64219 working the branch pick-up goods in October 1959. Passenger services on the branch had ceased in November 1951 and by 1959 Wragby was the railhead served by one daily freight from Lincoln, which in turn perished a year later.

With one exception the stations on the Bardney-Louth branch still survive and the former loop platform at Wragby is seen in May 1995. The roof of the platform building can just be seen above the tender of the 'J6' in the 'past' picture. With thanks to Mr & Mrs I. Swallow, who now own the Station House, for allowing access.
Mike Black/Roger Hill

LOUTH: On 9 May 1946 ex-Great Northern 'D2' 4-4-0 No 4383 stands in Louth station with a northbound freight. The former GN East Lincolnshire main line through Louth closed in October 1970 and a surviving single-line freight service from Grimsby to the Louth Maltings ceased in December 1980, thus completely erasing Louth from the railway map and leaving it as the largest town in Lincolnshire without trains.

By 1995 the station site has been completely redeveloped with industrial units and housing, although fortunately, after many years at the mercy of vandals, the magnificent station building is now listed and in the process of being converted into flats. *H. C. Casserley/Roger Hill*

WILLOUGHBY JUNCTION on the East Lincolnshire main line in March 1963, with 'B1' 4-6-0 No 61174 heading an up local, and a Derby-built DMU in the Mablethorpe bay platform.

Only the trackbed and the remnants of the up main platform survive at Willoughby in May 1995. *Mike Black/Roger Hill*

HAVENHOUSE station on the Skegness line on 19 April 1959, with a Class 31 diesel approaching on a Skegness-Boston empty stock train.
A Class 153 forms a Skegness-Nottingham service at the same location in April 1995. The station is still nominally open, although very few trains stop there; the signalling and crossing have been automated and the attractive gardens have long gone to seed. Surprisingly, however, the station still boasts a fully operational gents' toilet and five somersault signals survive elsewhere on the line. *J. Spencer Gilks/Roger Hill*

SPILSBY: No 64199 leaves Spilsby on 16 May 1954 with the RCTS railtour referred in the Bardney caption above. The Firsby-Spilsby branch closed completely in November 1958 and by April 1995 the only evidence of the railway there is the former goods shed, now in industrial use. *J. F. Oxley/Roger Hill*

BOSTON: Another 'J6', this time No 64244, leaves Boston past Grand Sluice crossing with a Sunday excursion to Skegness on 29 June 1952.

The same much-rationalised location on 28 June 1993 sees a pair of Class 20 diesels, Nos 20138 and 20066, bound for Skegness with the 0812 from Leicester. This was the last summer of this celebrated working, and apart from a very occasional special, loco-hauled services on this line are now extinct. *Les Perrin/Roger Hill*

SPALDING: The view south from the station on 22 September 1958 shows LMS Class '4' 2-6-0 No 43108 arriving off the former Midland & Great Northern Joint line with a train from Kings Lynn. The level crossing possessed two sets of gates, only one of which needed to be cleared at a given time, depending upon the movements required. At this time there were three other lines to the south of Spalding, the Great Northern & Great Eastern Joint to March, which diverged to the left south of the M&GN in this picture, the GN to Peterborough, and (to the right) the M&GN to Bourne.

The footbridge from which the 1958 picture was taken has been removed, but a broadly similar view is obtainable today from the signal box. The M&GN was closed completely by 1965, and the March line in 1982, leaving just the line to Peterborough and a simplified and modernised level crossing. On Spalding Flower Festival Day, 6 May 1995, Class 47 No 47704 approaches with the former Manchester Pullman stock, returning from servicing at Peterborough, prior to departing for Manchester. *John Foreman/John Hillier*

HIGH DYKE BRANCH: 'O2/1' No 63930 hammers up this mineral branch on 25 June 1960 with empty iron ore tipplers. The area was rich in ironstone and from the branch's construction in 1915 until gradual rundown in the 1960s, the quarries at Stainby and Colsterworth served the needs of steelworks all over the country via the sidings adjacent to the East Coast Main Line near Stoke Tunnel.

The steel industry in the 1990s imports the majority of its iron ore, and the High Dyke branch closed in August 1973. This is the view from the same section of embankment in March 1995; note the building on the horizon on the right and the shape of the tree just to the left of it in the middle distance, which serve to identify the location. *Hugh Ballantyne/Roger Hill*

GREAT PONTON station on the East Coast Main Line on 2 August 1958, with brand-new English Electric Type 4 (later Class 40) diesel No D207 heading an up express. Note the delightful lamps and the yard crane.

On 2 April 1995 a southbound IC 225 express passes the station site. The scene has changed greatly in 37 years, although the site of the former goods yard is still identifiable. *G. W. Morrison/John Hillier*